DPT

Draw It!

Woodland Animals

Patricia Walsh

Illustrations by David Westerfield

Heinemann Library
Chicago, Illinois

©2001 Reed Educational & Professional Publishing
Published by Heinemann Library,
an imprint of Reed Educational & Professional Publishing,
100 N. LaSalle, Suite 1010
Chicago, IL 60602
Visit our website at www.heinemannlibrary.com

Customer Service 888-454-2279

Designed by Meighan Depke
Illustrated by David Westerfield
Photos by Kim Saar
Printed in Hong Kong

05 04 03 02 01
10 9 8 7 6 5 4 3 2 1

Library of Congress Cataloging-in-Publication Data
Walsh, Patricia, 1951-
     Woodland animals / by Patricia Walsh ; illustrations by David Westerfield.
        p. cm. – (Draw it!)
     Summary: Instructions and illustrations demonstrate how to draw various wildlife from a North American forest habitat, including the bear, owl, and skunk.
     ISBN 1-57572-352-2
     1. Forest animals in art—Juvenile literature. 2. Drawing—Technique—Juvenile literature. [1. Animals in art. 2. Drawing—Technique.] I. Westerfield, David, 1956- ill. II. Title.

NC783.8.F67 W35 2000
743.6—dc21
                                            00-023385

Some words are shown in bold, **like this.** You can find out what they mean by looking in the glossary.

Contents

Introduction...4

Bear...6

Deer...8

Eagle...10

Fox...12

Mouse...14

Owl...16

Porcupine...18

Rabbit...20

Raccoon...22

Skunk...24

Squirrel...26

Woodpecker...28

Glossary...30

Art Glossary...31

More Books...32

Index...32

Introduction

Would you like to improve the pictures that you draw?

Well, you can! In this book, the artist has drawn pictures of woodland animals. He has used lines and shapes to draw each picture in small, simple steps. Follow these steps and your picture will come together for you too.

Here is advice from the artist:

- Always draw lightly at first.

- Draw all the shapes and pieces in the right places.

- Pay attention to the spaces between the lines as well as the lines themselves.

- Add details and **shading** to finish your drawing.

- And finally, erase the lines you don't need.

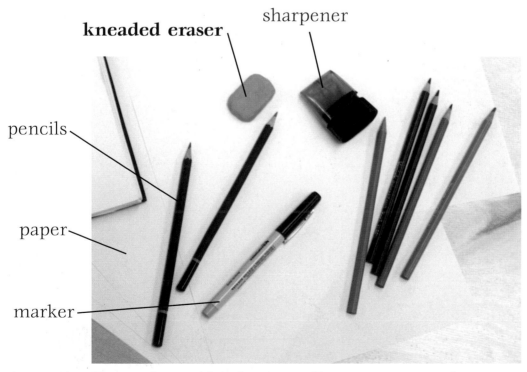

You only need a few supplies to get started.

There are four things you need for drawing:

- a pencil (medium or soft). You might also use
  a fine marker or pen to finish your drawing
- a pencil sharpener
- paper
- an eraser. A kneaded eraser works best. It can be
  squeezed into small or odd shapes. This eraser can
  also make pencil lines lighter without erasing them.

Now, are you ready? Do you have everything?
Then turn the page and let's draw!

*The drawings in this book were done by David Westerfield. David started drawing when he was very young. In college, he studied drawing and painting. Now he is a **commercial artist** who owns his own graphic design business. He has two children, and he likes to draw with them. David's advice to anyone who hopes to become an artist is, "Practice, practice, practice—and learn as much as you can from other artists."*

Draw a Bear

The black bear lives in the mountains throughout North America. It is a meat-eater, but it also eats berries, nuts, bark, and insects. It eats a lot of food in the summer to get ready for its deep winter sleep.

1 **Sketch** three slightly overlapping ovals. Make the first two ovals for the body larger than the third oval. These are your **guidelines**.

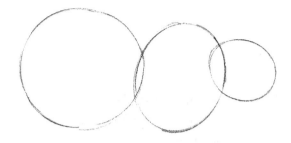

2 Connect the tops and bottoms of the three ovals with curved lines. Add a U-shaped **snout** to the small oval to shape the head.

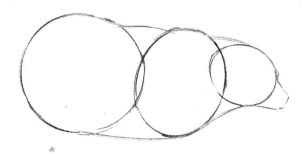

3 Draw two legs under each large oval. Use two smaller ovals connected by straight lines for each leg. End each leg with a short line and curve to begin the feet.

Add a mouth and nose on the snout. Draw an oval above the mouth for the eye. Add a dot in the center. Draw two half circles on top of the head for ears. Make some squiggly lines to show the fur.

Shape the four thick legs by drawing a line on either side of the leg ovals under the body. Connect the leg lines with a U shaped line at the bottom of each leg.

Erase the guidelines. To make the shaggy fur, **shade** the bear's body with short, soft pencil strokes. Add several pencil strokes around the bear's feet for grass.

Draw a Deer

The white-tailed deer lives almost everywhere in the United States. It has a thin, reddish summer coat and a dense, gray winter coat. The winter coat traps the deer's **body heat** so well that snow does not melt on a deer's back.

1 **Sketch** two ovals to make the **guidelines** for the body. Begin the deer's back and belly by drawing two lines to connect the ovals.

2 Sketch a smaller oval for the head above and to the right of the deer's body. Draw two curved lines to connect it to the body.

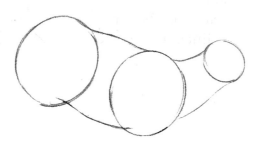

3 Begin the four legs by drawing one overlapping oval at the bottom of each body oval. Draw smaller ovals connected by straight lines below the body. To show the deer running, draw one leg stretched forward in front and the two legs bent upward in back.

4 Draw lines on either side of the leg ovals to shape each leg. Make a wedge-shaped hoof at the bottom of each leg.

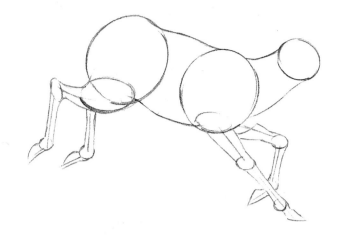

5 Add a triangle-shaped tail near the top of the first oval. Add a curved triangle near the top of the head for an ear. Add a U-shaped **snout** and a small oval for the eye. To add **antlers** for a male deer, sketch two S-shaped curves on top of the head and five or six short lines in the larger curves.

6 Draw a C-shape on the snout for the nose and **shade** in. Use short pencil strokes to make the deer's soft fur, but leave some white under the tail and on the belly, neck, and nose.

Draw an Eagle

The bald eagle is a **raptor**. The bald eagle is not bald at all but has a hood of white feathers. A young eagle is all brown. It gets its white head feathers and white tail feathers when it is five years old.

1 Draw a large oval for the body and a small oval for the head. Connect the ovals with one line across the top.

2 Begin the legs with two ovals that overlap the side of the body. Then draw a narrow leg and a strong foot with sharp, curved **talons** coming from each oval.

3 **Sketch** curved **guidelines** that swoop from the body for the outstretched wings. Make a circular tail guideline around the feet.

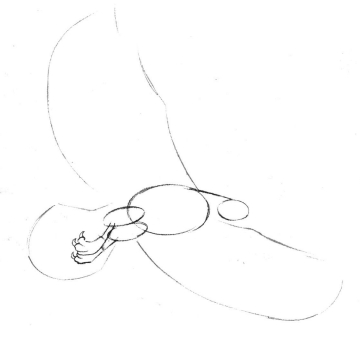

4 Add a jagged line to the left of the head to show the edge of the head feathers. On the head, draw a sharp, curved beak with an oval eye above it.

5 Draw a line along the top edge of the wing guidelines. Draw strong pointed feathers over the ends of the wing guidelines. Draw zig-zag lines for the feathered edges on the bottom of the wing. Make a zig-zag line along the tail guideline to show the tail feathers.

6 **Shade** using straight lines on the large wing and tail feathers. Shade the front part of the wings and the body with shorter strokes. Leave the eagle's head and tail feathers white. If you like, you can shade in some blue sky behind the eagle.

Draw a Fox

A red fox has a bushy red coat and a white-tipped tail. Its tail trails behind it as it trots along the forest edge. In winter, a sleeping fox uses its fluffy tail like a blanket to cover its feet and nose.

1 **Sketch** two ovals of the same size to make **guidelines** for the body. Connect the ovals with a line at the top and bottom.

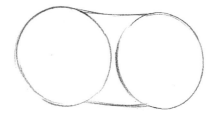

2 Draw a long line coming down from the top of the first oval and use a curved line below that to begin the tail. Draw a circle above the oval on the right for the head. Draw two short lines to connect it to the body. Make a U-shape to one side for the **snout**.

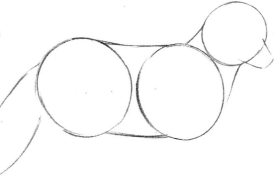

3 Draw two ovals that overlap the bottom of the body to begin the legs. Draw smaller ovals connected by straight lines for each leg. End each leg with a short line for the foot.

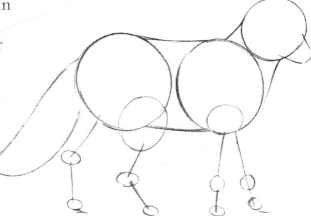

4 Draw a line on either side of each oval to shape the legs. Draw a wedge-shaped foot at the bottom of each foot.

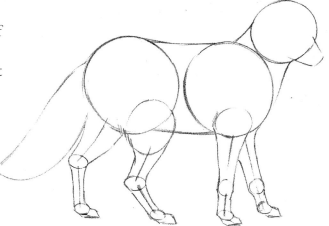

5 Add two triangular ears to the top of the head. Add an oval in the center of the head for an eye. **Shade** it in. Draw a small circle on the snout for the nose.

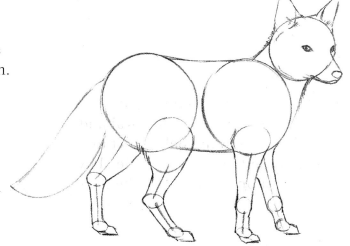

6 Use short pencil strokes to show the fox's fur. Shade the insides of the fox's legs and underneath the body. Leave the tail tip, belly, chest, and half of the face white. Shade the feet nearly black. Add a few short lines near the fox's feet for grass.

Draw a Mouse

A mouse is usually heard and seldom seen. A little rustling sound at night is often the only clue that a mouse is nearby. Mice eat seeds, leaves, grasses, bark, and buds. They usually hunt for food at night and hide underground during the day.

1 **Sketch** two overlapping egg-shaped ovals. Draw a circle around the lines where the egg-shapes overlap. These are the **guidelines** for the body and head.

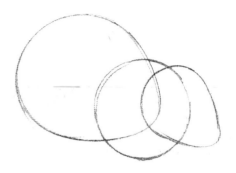

2 Mice have four legs, but only three can be seen in this drawing. Draw thick, straight lines under the body for legs. Make a rounded foot at each end.

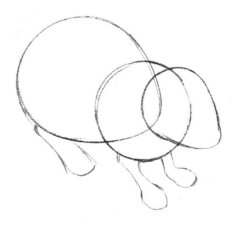

3 Draw an oval for each large ear. Divide the far ear with a short line. Draw a full round eye on the left side of the head and a smaller oval for the eye on the right side of the head.

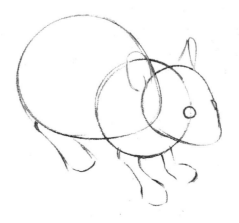

4 From the side of the largest egg-shape, draw two big U-shaped lines. Make the lines meet in a point to show the tail. Add zig-zag lines to each foot to make toes and tiny claws.

5 Reshape the top of the head to smooth the line to the body. Add a tiny line for the nose. Erase the guidelines that you no longer need.

6 Use short pencil strokes on the body and head to show the fur. Add several long lines to each side of the nose for whiskers. **Shade** the back of the body, the top of the head, the area beneath the neck, and a shadow on the ground. Draw a few oval seeds at the mouse's feet.

Draw an Owl

The great horned owl is a night-hunting raptor. It is called the "feathered tiger of the air" because it is one of the largest and fiercest owls. It eats rabbits and even chickens. The horns on its head are really feathers.

1 **Sketch** a large oval for the body. Draw a circle above it for the head. These are the **guidelines**.

2 Connect the head and body with two short lines. Add a large V for the tail. Draw two long curving **parallel** lines across the tail to make a branch.

3 Draw triangular shapes on the head for the feather horns. Draw two dark ovals for the eyes. Draw a straight line that slants up above each eye. Add a diamond shape between and a little below the eyes for the curved beak.

Draw two thick toes on the branch for each foot. Add a sharp, curved **talon** to each toe.

5 Draw a long, banana-like shape along the left side of the body for the wing. Sketch a W-shaped line over the the tail tip guideline and draw a large V in the center of the tail. Erase guidelines you no longer need.

6 Erase any tail and wing lines that overlap the branch. Then draw rows of short curved lines for body feathers. Draw face feathers with short lines that start below each eye. **Shade** the top of the head and the wings. Use the side of a pencil to darken parts of the branch.

Draw a Porcupine

The porcupine has long, rough hair for an outer coat. Under this coat are about 30,000 **quills**. When a porcupine is angry or in danger, it raises its quills. It does not throw them. Quills stick to any animal that touches them.

1 **Sketch** two ovals. Make one oval larger than the other. These are the **guidelines** for the body and head.

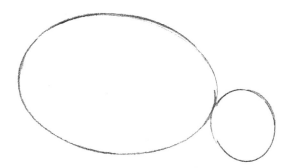

2 Add a large V on the left of the larger oval for the tail. Connect the tops of the large and small ovals with a short line. Draw a U-shaped **snout** at the bottom of the small oval.

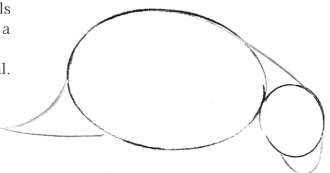

3 Draw two ovals that overlap the lower body. Sketch ovals connected by short lines below the body to begin the legs. Add tiny short lines at the bottom of each leg for the feet.

4 Draw lines on either side of the leg ovals to shape the short legs. Add sharp claws to each foot. Add a C-shape near the top of the head for an ear. Add a smaller circle inside it. Make a dark circle near the center of the head for an eye. Use a short curved line and short straight line to make the mouth and nose on the end of the snout.

5 Draw long, straight lines for the quills along the back from the top of the head to the tip and underside of the tail.

6 **Shade** the head with short lines. Add a few light lines to the sides of the snout for whiskers. Then fill in the body and tail with long lines pointing toward the back. Shade the legs. Make a few strokes back and forth with the side of the pencil to show the ground under the porcupine.

Draw a Rabbit

The cottontail rabbit is most active at dawn and dusk as it feeds on grasses. When it is frightened, it raises its tail to show the white underside. This tells other cottontails to dash for cover.

1   **Sketch** two overlapping ovals for the body. Add an overlapping circle near the top of the second oval for the head. These are the **guidelines**.

2   Begin the back legs by drawing one oval on the body. Draw two ovals below it for back feet. Connect the foot on the left side to the oval using two short lines. For the front legs, draw a smaller oval on the front of the body. Draw two small ovals for front feet under the body. Then connect the feet to the body with three lines.

3   Add two long ears to the top of the head. Make the tips round. Add a wide U-shape to the front of the head for a **snout**. At the back of the body, add a very short line that ends in an oval tail.

4 Draw a pointed oval near the center of the head for a large eye. Make tiny short lines around the eye. Draw two short lines on the snout for a nose and a mouth. Add a few short whiskers from the snout and a few short lines inside the ear.

5 Draw darker lines to smooth out the guidelines you used for the body and legs. Draw one or two short lines on each paw to show toes.

6 Use short, light pencil strokes for the soft fur. **Shade** the back of the body, head, and ears. Leave the inside of the left ear, a space around the eye and nose, and its cottontail white. Use a few short pencil strokes around the rabbit's feet to show grass.

Draw a Raccoon

The raccoon has dark rings on its tail and a dark mask across its face. It is mostly **nocturnal**, but you might see a raccoon raiding a trash can in the early morning or evening.

1 **Sketch** two overlapping ovals. Add an overlapping circle to the right of the second oval. These are the **guidelines**.

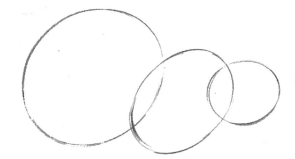

2 Connect the tops and bottoms of the ovals and circle with curved lines. Add a V-shaped **snout** to the side of the circle. Draw a long swoop at one end of the body for a tail.

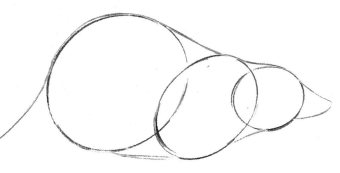

3 Add a long, curved line below the tail line. Draw curved and straight lines below the body ovals to begin the legs. Add short, squiggly lines at the left side of the head, on the back of the legs, and under the body.

4 Add two triangle shapes to the top of the head for ears. Add a dark oval for the eye. Make a circle on the end of the snout for a nose. Make the raccoon's mask by drawing a U-shape across its face around the eye. Darken an area at the bottom of the head.

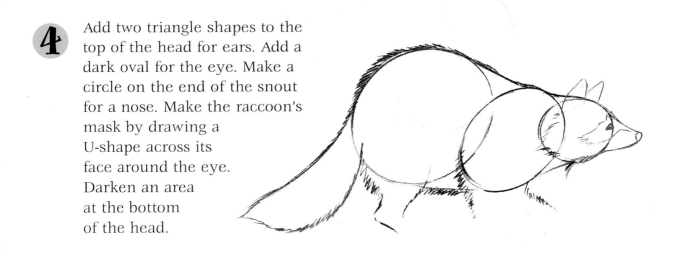

5 Draw the top of the back leg with two curving lines on the rear of the body. Draw small ovals and lines on either side to shape the front and back legs. Make wedge-shaped feet at the bottom of each leg.

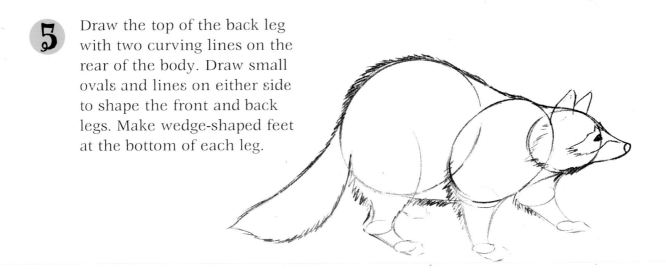

6 Darken the mask and add a few whisker lines from the snout. **Shade** five or six dark rings on the tail. Use short lines to draw toes on each foot. Use short pencil strokes to show the fur on the head, legs, and body.

Draw a Skunk

The striped skunk is an animal that can be found all over North America. It eats insects and small **rodents.** It defends itself by spraying a foul-smelling liquid called "musk." Its greatest enemies are automobiles and great horned owls.

1 **Sketch** two overlapping ovals. Make the second one larger than the first. Add a rounded triangular shape to the left of the first oval. These are the **guidelines** for the head and body.

2 Draw lines to connect the tops and bottoms of the three shapes. Add a plume-like tail to the largest oval. Make the tail in the shape of a large, thick C.

3 Sketch two small ovals on the body. To begin the legs, draw more ovals below the body. Connect these smaller ovals to the body with straight lines. Draw a short line at the bottom of each leg to show feet.

4 Draw curved lines on either side of the small ovals to outline the legs. Round off the bottoms of the feet. Draw sharp claws on each foot.

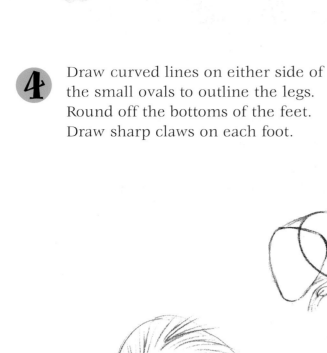

5 Add two dark dots to the head for eyes. Make the tail fluffy by outlining it with long lines. Use shorter lines to outline the head, legs, and body

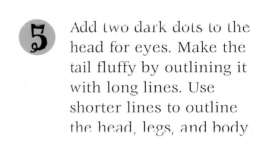

6 Add two shapes like small, upside-down Us to the head for ears. **Shade** the head and body. Leave white for the stripe along the side of its body and along its tail. Shade in an area under the skunk's body to show the ground.

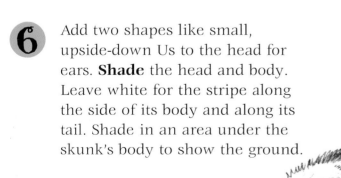

Draw a Squirrel

A tree squirrel is actually a **rodent** that is related to beavers and mice. In the fall, it buries nuts to use as food in the winter, but it does not really remember where it put the nuts. It uses its keen sense of smell to find its hidden food.

1 **Sketch** a big oval. Then sketch a second, smaller oval above and to the right of the first oval. These are the **guidelines** for the body and head.

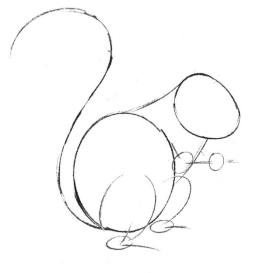

2 Connect the ovals with two slightly curved lines. Add a large S-curve that begins at the bottom of the larger oval as a guideline for the tail.

3 Start the tops of the back legs with two large ovals that overlap the body. Use short straight lines and ovals to make guidelines for all four legs. Draw the front legs above the back legs.

4 Draw curved lines on either side of the small ovals to outline the legs. Draw feet with claws on the ends of the toes. Draw an oval shape between the front feet for an acorn.

5 Smooth out the top of the squirrel's head. Add two triangles to the top of the head for ears. **Shade** in an oval for the eye in the center of the head. Add a curved line above and below the eye. Extend the side of the head with a curved line. Add a U-shaped **snout**. Use the tail guideline to help you draw a thick S-shape for the tail.

6 Fluff the tail by outlining it with long, soft pencil strokes. Shade the body, but leave the belly and bottom half of the face white. Darken the acorn and shade a patch of ground under the squirrel's feet.

Draw a Woodpecker

The downy woodpecker is the smallest of the eastern woodpeckers. Its feathers are black and white. It has a small red patch on the back of its head. Its bill makes a loud tapping noise as this bird pecks at trees to find insects.

1 Sketch a large oval with a smaller one on top. Draw two long **parallel** lines next to the first oval for a thick tree trunk.

2 Connect the head to the body with two short lines. Draw a curved line on the larger oval to start the wing. Add a straight line almost in the middle of the woodpecker's body. Make two V-shapes at the bottom of the wing. These are the wingtips.

3 Draw several thin V-shapes coming from the wing onto the tree for the tail.

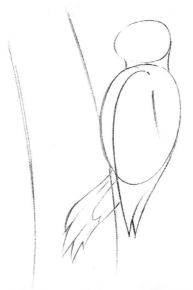

4 To make the foot, draw a thick X on the tree next to the body. Then draw a sharp **talon** on each end. Add **crosshatching** to the foot. Attach the foot to the body with a U-shape.

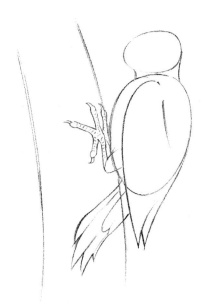

5 Draw a V on the side of the head for the **bill.** Divide it with a straight line. Add a dark circle on the head for the eye. Draw wiggly lines from the eye and the bill to the back of the head.

6 Add long, **vertical** lines going down the wing. Then cross those lines with short **horizontal** lines. **Shade** the wings, but leave bands of white. Shade the tail and three long patches on the head. Add a spot of red near the top of the head. Leave the chest and back white. Shade in the tree trunk.

Glossary

antler hornlike growth on the head of some animals

bill hard part of a bird's jaws; a beak

body heat warmth that comes from an animal or a person's skin

commercial artist person who designs and illustrates things for other people

nocturnal active during nighttime

quill stiff, sharp, hollow growth on a porcupine

raptor bird that hunts and kills other animals for food

rodent small, gnawing animal with sharp teeth

snout part of an animal's head that includes the nose, mouth, and jaws

talon claw of an animal that eats other animals or insects

Art Glossary

crosshatching
marking that uses lines that cross each other

guideline
light line, used to shape a drawing, that is usually erased in the final drawing.

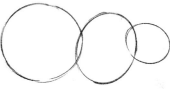

horizontal
line that is flat and level

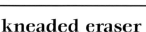

kneaded eraser
soft, squeezable eraser used to soften dark pencil lines

parallel
straight lines that lie next to one another but never touch

shade
make darker than the rest

sketch
draw quickly and roughly

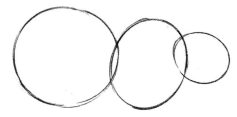

vertical
line that is straight up and down

More Books

Books about Drawing

Birch, Linda. *How to Draw & Paint Animals in Pencil, Charcoal, Line, & Watercolor.* New York: Sterling Publishing Co., Inc., 1997.

Cortina Famous Schools Staff. *How to Draw Animals.* New York: Holt, Henry & Co., 1995.

Parramon Editorial Team Staff. *Animals.* Hauppage, N.Y.: Barron's Educational Series, Inc., 1997.

Books about Woodland Animals

Carroll, Colleen. *How Artists See Animals: Mammal Fish Bird Reptile.* New York: Abbeville Press, Incorporated, 1996.

Fisher, Ron. *Cottontails: Little Rabbits of Field and Forest.* Washington, D.C.: National Geographic Society, 1997.

Parker, Barbara Keevil. *North American Wolves.* Minneapolis: Lerner Publishing Group, 1998.

Tracqui, Valerie. *The Brown Bear.* Madison, Wis.: Demco Media, 1998.

Weidensaul, Scott. *National Audubon Society First Field Guides: Birds.* New York: Scholastic, 1998.

Index

bald eagle 10–11

black bear 6–7

cottontail rabbit 20–21

downy woodpecker 28–29

drawing

  advice 4, 31

  tools 5

great horned owl 16, 24

mouse 14–15

North America 6, 24

porcupine 18–19

raccoon 22–23

raptor 10, 16

red fox 12–13

skunk 24–25

tree squirrel 26–27

United States 8

white-tailed deer 8–9